LetterNova

ABC: Global Foods

Written and illustrated by
J.C. Waylon

Leaf & Compass Publishing

LetterNova: ABC Global Foods
An imprint of Leaf & Compass Publishing
Written and illustrated by J.C. Waylon

Published by Leaf & Compass Publishing
Printed independently

ISBN: 979-8-9952221-6-3

“Life is like food—the more flavors you try, the richer it becomes.”

A - Arepas

Arepas are warm corn cakes loved in many places. They cook golden outside and soft inside. Each tasty bite feels like a happy hello.

B- Bunny Chow

Bunny Chow is bread filled
with warm curry.
It is served as a hearty meal
in South Africa.
Each scoop of flavor feels
bold and exciting.

C- Croissant

Croissants are flaky pastries with buttery layers.
They are baked golden and warm in ovens.
Each crisp bite crumbles into morning joy.

D - Dumplings

Dumplings are soft pockets filled with tasty surprises. They can be steamed, boiled, or fried to enjoy. Each little bundle opens with delicious wonder.

E - Eggs Benedict

Eggs Benedict is a warm breakfast with eggs and toast.
It is topped with creamy sauce and rich flavor.
Golden bites make the morning feel special.

F - Fried Chicken

Fried Chicken is a crispy meal loved around the world. It cooks golden outside with juicy meat inside. Crunchy bites bring happy smiles to the table.

G - Gyro

Gyro is a warm wrap filled with sliced meat.
It is tucked in soft bread with sauce and vegetables.
Savory flavors make every bite exciting.

H - Haggis

Haggis is a hearty dish from Scotland.
It is cooked warm with spices and rich flavor.
Its cozy taste brings comfort on chilly days.

▌- Injera

Injera is a soft flatbread
from Ethiopia.
It is spread wide and shared
with many dishes.
Its warm layers turn meals
into gatherings.

J - Jollof Rice

Jollof Rice is a bright dish
full of rich flavor.
It is cooked with rice,
tomatoes, and spices.
Its colorful steam fills the
table with joy.

K- Kebab

Kebab is a savory food cooked on skewers.
It is grilled with meat and vegetables over fire.
Smoky flavors make every meal feel festive.

L- Lamb Chops

Lamb Chops are tender cuts cooked with rich flavor. They sizzle on grills and plates around the world. Juicy bites make dinner feel special.

M - Mochi

Mochi is a soft treat made from rice.
It is chewy, smooth, and shaped into little rounds.
Sweet bites bounce with playful joy.

N - Nshima

Nshima is a warm cornmeal dish loved in Zambia. It is served soft and shared with many meals. Its simple comfort brings families together.

O - Oxtail

Oxtail is a rich dish cooked low and slow.
It becomes tender in warm sauce and spices.
Deep flavors make the table feel cozy.

P - Pho

Pho is a warm noodle soup
from Vietnam.
It is filled with broth, herbs,
and tender noodles.
Fragrant steam rises with
comforting flavor.

Q- Quesadilla

Quesadilla is a warm tortilla
filled with melted cheese.
It is folded crisp and cooked
until golden.
Cheesy slices bring smiles
with every pull.

R- Ravioli

Ravioli are pasta pockets filled with tasty goodness. They are cooked soft and covered with warm sauce. Tender bites turn dinner into delight.

S - Sushi

Sushi is a colorful food made with rice and fillings.
It is rolled neatly with fish or vegetables inside.
Beautiful bites make meals feel like art.

T - Tacos

Tacos are crunchy or soft shells filled with flavor. They hold meats, beans, cheese, and fresh toppings. Every taco brings a party to the plate.

U - Upside-Down Cake

Upside-Down Cake is a sweet
dessert baked with fruit.
It is flipped to show a bright
golden top.
Its surprise finish makes
dessert extra fun.

V - Vanilla Ice Cream

Vanilla Ice Cream is a cold treat with creamy sweetness. It is scooped smooth into bowls and cones. Cool swirls melt into smiles on warm days.

W - Wings

Wings are tasty bites loved
in many places.
They can be baked, fried, or
covered in sauce.
Bold flavors make snack
time exciting.

X - Xi Gua Lao

Xi Gua Lao is a cool watermelon dessert from China.
It is smooth, sweet, and served chilled.
Refreshing spoonfuls feel like summer in a bowl.

Y - Yams

Yams are hearty roots cooked in many ways. They can be roasted, mashed, or baked until soft. Warm bites bring comfort to every meal.

Z - Zebra Cake

Zebra Cake is a sweet treat
with striped layers.
It is baked with swirls of
chocolate and vanilla.
Fun slices bring smiles with
every stripe.

Explore The Letternova Series

www.ingramcontent.com/pod-product-compliance
Ingram Content Group UK Ltd.
Pitfield, Milton Keynes, MK11 3LW, UK
UKHW061950290726
14090UKWH00021B/1169